DEALING WITH DESIRES YOU CAN'T CONTROL
by Mark R. McMinn, Ph.D.

A MINISTRY OF THE NAVIGATORS
P.O. BOX 6000, COLORADO SPRINGS, CO 80934

The Navigators is an international Christian organization. Jesus Christ gave His followers the Great Commission to go and make disciples (Matthew 28:19). The aim of The Navigators is to help fulfill that commission by multiplying laborers for Christ in every nation.

NavPress is the publishing ministry of The Navigators. NavPress publications are tools to help Christians grow. Although publications alone cannot make disciples or change lives, they can help believers learn biblical discipleship, and apply what they learn to their lives and ministries.

Third printing, 1990

A portion of the content of this booklet is adapted from _Your Hidden Half_ by Mark R. McMinn, published by Baker Book House (1988). Used by permission.

All Scripture quotations in this publication are from the _Holy Bible: New International Version_ (NIV). Copyright © 1973, 1978, 1984, International Bible Society. Used by permission of Zondervan Bible Publishers.

Printed in the United States of America

FOR A FREE CATALOG OF
NAVPRESS BOOKS & BIBLE STUDIES,
CALL TOLL FREE 1-800-366-7788 (USA)
or 1-416-499-4615 (CANADA)

DEALING WITH DESIRES YOU CAN'T CONTROL

Mike is a happily married business executive, committed to his family. He knows that marital infidelity leads to a host of problems including lack of trust, communication difficulties, and insecurity. But Mike is attracted to his close friend Janice. Sometimes Mike is preoccupied with Janice while sitting at his desk trying to complete paperwork. He is distracted. His job performance is suffering, he is more irritable with his children, and his wife wonders what has happened to the marriage. He enjoys the feelings of attraction, but is tired of the struggle. How can he cope? Mike is experiencing temptation. His well-reasoned commitment to his marriage is in conflict with his impulse to make inappropriate advances toward Janice.

Not everyone faces the same temptation as Mike, but all of us face temptations of one sort or another. We all experience conflicts

3

between what we want to do as committed Christians and what we want to do as biological human beings. Even the Apostle Paul described the struggle with temptation in personal terms: "I do not understand what I do. For what I want to do I do not do, but what I hate I do" (Romans 7:15). Temptation haunts us at every age: riddling us as children, devastating us as adolescents, confusing us as adults. So we live our lives in conflict: wondering how much to spend on the new car or how fast to drive on the freeway or how much lasagna to take when offered second helpings.

The key is not *eliminating* temptation, but *managing* temptation. For example, pretend you're on a diet. After you finish your chef salad with low-cal Italian dressing, the waiter returns with a tray of sumptuous desserts. You have an impulse to eat dessert but your well-reasoned side insists on abstinence. How likely is it that any kind of self-management strategy will *eliminate* that conflict? Not very! The most you can hope for is *managing* the temptation. Later that night, as your stomach growls in front of the television set, you recognize both the difficulty of losing weight and the value of self-discipline. Despite your hunger, you feel good about your decision to manage the impulse.

Trying to eliminate temptation makes it harder to manage. The converse is also true: managing temptation is easier after shedding the unrealistic expectation that it can be

4

eliminated. Suppose Mike concludes that his temptation cannot be eliminated. He might begin to look more closely at his experience rather than desperately scrambling for recipe-like answers. In exploring his feelings and investigating his motives, he might begin to understand more fully the meaning of marital fidelity, the devastating consequences of infidelity, and the value of commitment to moral standards. He will learn more about grace and love and pain. He will grow. Denying that the temptation exists makes it grow stronger. Managing temptation produces growth and godliness.

Trying to Eliminate Temptation Makes It Grow Stronger

If we pretend temptation doesn't exist, it comes in greater force and we are unprepared. Some conclude we should "just say no" to temptation. But it's not always that easy! Mike can try just saying "no" to temptation. He might try cold showers every morning and evening. He might become more involved in family or church activities to distract him from Janice. But these strategies won't remove the temptation. Distraction techniques may work for a time, but the impulses will fight back. The impulses will have to become stronger to fight back. They probably will be.

We all experience impulses—the desire to act rashly. Some people have impulses to spend money unwisely, others impulsively desire drugs or excessive alcohol, others struggle to control their anger or eating behaviors. In good decision making, impulses are filtered through sound reasoning. Impulsive decisions are dangerous.

Impulse comes in two forms. Most of us recognize urges from the old, carnal nature as impulses. I call these "dark side" impulses. Less recognized are the impulses from the part of our personalities that wants to look good to others. I call these "glossy side" impulses. The dark side and the glossy side work together, making temptation strong and difficult to fight.

The dark side
The dark side of impulse is egocentric, focusing on self. Like psychoanalyst Carl Jung's concept of "shadow," the dark side seeks pleasure and avoids pain. Jung's personality theory must be interpreted cautiously by Christians since he derived much of his theory from readings in the occult, alchemy, and parapsychology. Nonetheless, his "shadow" is an undeniable part of human personality, consistent with the Christian doctrine of fallen nature. The dark side is irrational and considers none of the constraints of reality. Mike's attraction to Janice is a result of a dark side impulse.

You may wonder, "Doesn't Mike care about his wife and his children?" Actually Mike cares a great deal about family life, but he is so preoccupied with the dark side impulse that he overlooks his family. Impulses from the dark side are egocentric, seek immediate gratification, and avoid responsibility.

The human capacity for dark side impulses—including aggressiveness and sexual immorality—is mind-boggling. Fifty-five million people were killed during World War II alone, with Hitler killing up to six thousand Jews per day. Plotless films filled with automatic weapons and needless destruction fill theaters and break box office records. One in ten women will be assaulted by her spouse at some point in her marriage. Those women who finally press charges will have been attacked an average of thirty-five times! As early as the 1940s, one researcher found that thirty-seven percent of males had experienced a homosexual encounter. The results may have been upwardly biased, but it points to wide-range sexual confusion, even forty years ago. A 1983 study showed that over forty percent of married adults had been sexually unfaithful to their spouses. Can we even begin to estimate how many others have sexual conflicts with pornography? How many, like Mike, have secret attractions to coworkers, causing personal conflict? Dark side impulses are common and powerful.

The glossy side
Impulses from the glossy side come from that part of a person's personality that always wants to look good in public. Jesus Christ confronted

the religious leaders of His day many times about their excessive desire for respect and approval from others. The Pharisees were ruled by glossy side impulses. Because Mike believes good Christians don't face sexual temptation like his, he keeps his battle private, constantly fearing what others would think if he were discovered. He wraps his fragile self-image in the glossy public self he presents to others.

The glossy side may first appear to be quite pious, but a closer look reveals its impulsive nature. Just as an animal can learn morality based on avoiding punishment, we can learn to *appear* spiritual in order to avoid disapproval from other Christians. The glossy side looks for easy answers, is quick to judge others, and sets up arbitrary standards for spirituality.

The glossy side is far from righteous because it so centrally focuses on self and not on the broader dimensions of God's truth. Again, the Pharisees are a good example. Their pseudo righteousness was the result of glossy side impulses. They wanted others to notice their piety and to respect their spiritual positions. True righteousness is not motivated by the glossy side, but by a desire to honor God even if people don't notice or absolutely reject godliness. Glossy side righteousness is a self-centered form of piety far from God's notion of spirituality. True spirituality focuses on God rather than on self.

A vicious combination

The dark side and the glossy side are a vicious combination; the two combined are far more dangerous than either one alone. Dark side impulses evoke glossy side impulses. Whenever Mike feels attraction toward Janice, he feels tremendous guilt and tells himself that "good Christians don't face temptations like this." Similarly, glossy side impulses evoke dark side impulses. Whenever Mike tells himself that "good Christians aren't attracted to other women," he becomes overwhelmed with his attraction toward Janice. The dark side and the glossy side feed each other. As one grows so does the other, and the result is hypocrisy and duality—a battle of impulses. The Lord Jesus saw this pattern among the Pharisees (Matthew 23:27), and the Apostle Paul noted it in the early Church (Colossians 2:20-23). Robert Louis Stevenson fictionalized the syndrome with *The Strange Case of Dr. Jekyll and Mr. Hyde*, in which Jekyll was the upstanding citizen and Hyde was his secret and evil alter ego. We still see the pattern today.

In *The Empire Strikes Back*, the great Jedi master Yoda is training Luke Skywalker to become a Jedi knight. The young Skywalker fears the dark side will become too strong if not destroyed immediately, and he feels drawn to fight a symbolic battle with it in a nearby cave. Entering the cave with light-saber drawn, the would-be Jedi faces the evil Darth

Vader. Luke lops off Vader's head during a brief fight. But as Vader's black helmet lies on the ground, Skywalker's own face gradually appears beneath the face shield. Has Luke killed part of himself?

Potential evil is as dissonant for us as it is for Skywalker in the movie fantasy. We want to destroy evil and live in spiritual peace. We want to remove temptation and live in clarity. So we take up our swords impulsively to purge evil by destroying it. We use arbitrary "shoulds" and seek easy answers. We strike down temptation and feel immediate relief, but gradually we become aware that we have tried to eliminate a part of ourselves that cannot be done away with—a part that only returns with greater force. In the process of trying to eliminate temptation, we short-circuit growth. Trying to eliminate temptation makes it grow stronger.

Self-deprivation is a frequent glossy side response to temptation. One man who sought counseling was addicted to video pornography. I was interested that he didn't own a television because, as he said, "Jesus would never watch the garbage on network television." He also felt immediate guilt whenever he found a woman attractive. He was trying to control his behavior by self-deprivation. It's not an uncommon pattern. Ironically, it's often the one who believes all anger is wrong that ends up exploding violently with the children. It's often the one who sells the television that ends up watching pornography on a rented television. The dieter who tries to live on celery and carrot sticks often ends up eating a half-gallon of ice cream and a double cheese pizza. Self-deprivation is an ineffective way of dealing with temptation because it intensifies our focus on the thing we are attempting to avoid. (Try this experiment: For the next five minutes, do everything you can to avoid thinking about pink elephants.)

> Since you died with Christ to the basic principles of this world, why, as though you still belonged to it, do you submit to its rules: "Do not handle! Do not taste! Do not touch!"? These are all destined to perish with use, because they are based on human commands and teachings. Such regulations indeed have an appearance of wisdom, with their self-imposed worship, their false humility and their harsh treatment of the body, but they lack any value in restraining sensual indulgence. (Colossians 2:20-23)

Trying to Manage Temptation Brings It Under Control

We cannot destroy dark side impulses; they are part of our human experience. But we can understand and then manage our temptations. An important first step is affirming that temptation is not sin.

Temptation is not sin.

If Christians were surveyed, most would say temptation is not sin, but that giving in to temptation with inappropriate thoughts or actions is sin. Jesus was tempted (Mark 1:12-13), yet He was without sin. Therefore temptation is not sin.

But our reactions and our theology may be incongruent. If we could take those same Christians and put "guilt-meters" on their foreheads, we might be intrigued by the results. In the presence of temptation, many meters would register significant guilt feelings. The glossy side thoughts that produce guilt feelings are predictable: "Good Christians aren't tempted in the ways I'm tempted." "If I were focusing on the Lord, I wouldn't be struggling with strong temptations." "If others knew about this temptation, I would be asked to resign from the church leadership committee." And so on. These thoughts are based on approval-seeking and arbitrary rules without biblical basis. The Bible never presents temptation as sin.

Temptation can be used for evil or good. If temptation causes sin, then the outcome is clearly evil. But temptation can instead be productive:

> Consider it pure joy, my brothers, when-
> ever you face trials of many kinds,
> because you know that the testing
> of your faith develops perseverance.
> Perseverance must finish its work

so that you may be mature and complete, not lacking anything. (James 1:2-4)

The same Greek word translated "trials" in verse 2 is translated "temptation" in verse 13. The source of temptation is internal (verses 13-14)—from within our character—but that temptation can be used to produce growth.

If temptation is viewed as evil, we will respond by trying to eliminate rather than manage it. The result is a battle of internal impulses that actually makes the temptation stronger. The more Mike tries to push the temptations from his mind, the more impulsive and irresponsible he becomes.

In the midst of lessons on Christian devotion, purity, and commitment, our Christian teaching often communicates subtle messages about non-temptation. We easily start thinking that the best Christians are never tempted. Because Christians are well-trained at hiding temptation, many are left feeling alone and unspiritual. Temptation is fertile in the private life of one who cannot discuss it with Christian friends. Temptation plus isolation often produces sin.

When we do see the dark side of another, we are often so shocked that we respond reflexively. Gordon McDonald resigned his Christian leadership position when his past infidelity became known, even though he had undergone a period of supervised restoration. He knew how

Christians would respond. We rightly expect purity in our Christian leaders, but our shocked reaction to sin can be excessive. If we allowed the open discussion of temptation and sin, we could learn lessons from sincere Christians who have remorsefully acknowledged their errors. God can use broken servants when we allow Him to. Remember King David.

Of course we strive for purity, and we don't want to become so comfortable with temptation that we compromise our zeal for righteousness. Paul instructed Timothy to flee temptation. But some temptation seems flee-resistant. Feeling guilty or sinful about these strong temptations is not the answer.

Mike's temptation would be more easily managed if he discussed it with a trustworthy Christian friend. Scripture reminds us to "carry each other's burdens" (Galatians 6:2). We would all do well to have one person with whom we can be completely accountable. For some, a spouse can play this role. Others seek a close personal friend or a Christian counselor.

Recognize that life is difficult.
A second step in managing temptation involves recognizing that life always will be filled with trials and difficulties. Giving in to temptation, in a sense, is an attempt to escape the difficulty of life. Because it is difficult to remain faithful in marriage, many resort to secret relationships. Because it is difficult to cope with children who spill milk twice in one

meal, some resort to verbal or physical child abuse. Because it is difficult to cope with hectic schedules and impoverished self-esteems, many resort to substance abuse, seeking to make life more bearable.

Tragically, efforts to make life less difficult end up making it more difficult. Secret relationships eventually produce marital crises, verbal abuse produces defiant children, and substance abuse produces greater life stress and poorer self-esteem. As M. Scott Peck concluded his book *The Road Less Traveled*, accepting life as difficult makes life more bearable. It also makes temptation less powerful.

Articles and books on effective Christian living are often very insightful and significant, but we must be cautious not to communicate that Christianity is a "Band-Aid" for all emotional hurts. Some things in life are meant to be difficult, and no easy answer will remove the pain. In an essay on intellect, Ralph Waldo Emerson wrote, "God offers to every mind a choice between truth and repose. Take which you please, you can never have both." Life is difficult.

God's amazing grace
Perhaps the most powerful tool in managing temptation is God's grace. His grace is an unconditional love and empowering presence that allows us to face the trials of life with the presence of the living God. Grace

makes love unconditional, pain bearable, and hope substantive. When Paul was discouraged about his tendency to give in to temptation in Romans 7, he responded by recalling God's grace: "Therefore, there is now no condemnation for those who are in Christ Jesus, because through Christ Jesus the law of the Spirit of life set me free from the law of sin and of death" (Romans 8:1-2).

Grace and impulse are completely incompatible. Impulse—whether from the dark side or the glossy side—focuses on self. Grace transcends self because it comes from God and we don't deserve it. Understanding grace forces us to let go of our proud independence, drawing us to a deeper reliance on God and His provision for our every need.

Many of us speak of grace as if we understand it, but we live by investing effort in *earning* God's favor, condemning ourselves when we fail, and focusing on how evil our hidden desires are. In other words, we try *earning* God's grace rather than *responding* to God's grace. David Seamands, in his excellent book *Healing for Damaged Emotions*, wrote,

> We read, we hear, we believe a good theology of grace. But that's not the way we live. We believe grace in our heads but not in our gut level feelings or in our relationships. There's no other word we throw around so piously.[1]

We talk about grace, but sometimes attempt to understand it with impulsive thinking. Glossy side impulses escalate and self-defeating guilt results. *Grace must be separated from personal performance in order to understand it.* God doesn't want us to glory in our accomplishments or moan in our inadequacies. We can't be justified by earning His favor. He doesn't value us because of our performance. "For it is by grace you have been saved, through faith—and this not from yourselves, it is the gift of God" (Ephesians 2:8).

It doesn't matter much whether we're worthless or worthwhile. It is more significant that God's love doesn't depend on our value. We are free to respond to His unconditional grace rather than being bound to earn His favor. That's why understanding grace is so important in managing temptation. Because we all have an old nature, we inevitably fail. Responding to failure becomes important in avoiding future battles of impulse. When we fully understand grace, we respond differently to failure. Rather than focusing on self ("I'm such a bad Christian"), we focus on God ("It is amazing that God loves me despite my tendency toward evil"). It's His truth that sets us free.

Choosing the good life

After considering that temptation is not sin, recognizing that life is difficult, and freshly appreciating God's grace, Mike is still left with a choice. Hopefully, he will choose to do right and to grow in response to his temptation rather than giving in to his battle of impulses—the dark side versus the glossy side.

Tragically, many people make bad choices looking for the "good life." They want the pleasure and fun for which the dark side yearns. But impulsive choices lead to anything but a good life. Those living by impulse end up in a complex web of broken relationships, defeated emotions, and shallow spirituality. They seek the good life and end up miserable.

If Mike makes a good choice, in obedience to God's gracious guidance, he will be choosing God's "good life." It's a *difficult* life filled with temptation and struggles, but a *good* life of obedience, purity, and opportunities for growth.

Asking the important questions
Because temptation is uncomfortable, we naturally think it can be escaped. But trying to destroy dark side impulses intensifies glossy side impulses, fertilizes the battle of impulses, and makes self-focus a way of life. In the midst of the battles we can't see grace. The bigger picture is obscured as the rigid rules of the glossy side battle the "wants" of the dark side. Trying to eliminate temptation only makes it stronger.

When temptation comes, it's not enough to tread water, to try to hold our own in Christian living. Temptation is an opportunity to forge ahead, to grow in our understanding of God. Mike has a chance for growth. By not giving in to dark side impulses or glossy side impulses, he can ask more important questions: "How can this temptation help me better understand God's commitment to His bride, the Church?" "How can this struggle be used for good in my spiritual pilgrimage?" "How can I better understand the nature of marital commitment because of this temptation?" To answer these questions, we have to get beyond our natural inclination to cover up the dark side with glossy side answers.

Instead, we must consider it joy when we encounter temptations because God is using them to drive us back to Him. We must also deepen our accountability relationships, rely less on ourselves, reduce our subtle pride, identify areas of need, and renew our commitment to godly obedience. Those who survive major temptation without giving in to sin are stronger than they were before the temptation came.

We need more Christians who live obediently in the midst of temptation not because of a list of rules, but because they respond to God's limitless grace. Because God accepts us and loves us despite our sin, we know His grace doesn't depend on our performance. We can be whole before God, assured of His love. Recognizing our completeness in God gives us peace and enables us to act with consistent obedience. It allows us to focus on God, to look beyond the unworthiness of humankind, and to accept others openly. Temptation can become a stepping stone to greater understanding and wholeness.

Summary
Trying to eliminate temptation makes it grow stronger, as dark and glossy side impulses battle and focus us on ourselves. By contrast, trying to manage temptation brings it under control. Managing temptation includes:

- becoming convinced that temptation is not sin, and discussing it with a trusted friend;
- recognizing that life is difficult;
- depending on God's grace rather than our performance to feel loved;
- choosing the good life of purity and growth over the false "good life" of pleasure; and
- asking the important questions that lead to growth.

For Reflection and Action

1. What persistent area of temptation is currently causing you the most concern?

Give in to my anger (mostly toward kids or my dad)

2. What is your glossy side—that part that wants to look perfect to others—telling you to do about this area of temptation?

Be sweet & nice - try to look as though you have infinite patience.

3. How likely is it that you can completely eliminate this area of temptation from your life? *not likely*

4. How might this temptation cause you to grow and better know God and His grace? (Name as many ways as possible.)

Each time I'm tempted I must look to God for help. — I can understand others in similar circ; — I can understand How God must be grieved at me yet shows me compassion — I should also do for my kids

5. How does it make you feel to know God loves you despite your temptations (and failures) in this area of your life? *It floods me with gratitude & praise because it amazes me!*

6. Why is responding to God's grace more important than trying to earn God's favor?

It brings us into proper relationship w/ Him, & relieves us of a life of guilt. This is how He chooses to teach us.

7. Talk with God about this area of temptation. Tell Him all about your feelings, what your dark and glossy sides are each telling you, and what you think Scripture says about it. If you've already fallen, confess this to God and believe that He forgives you. Ask Him for the grace to resist the temptation. Talk with Him about possible underlying motives

and anything else He might be trying to teach you through this experience.

For Meditation

Read one of the following passages several times a day, and think about what it means for your life.

> *No temptation has seized you except what is common to man. And God is faithful; he will not let you be tempted beyond what you can bear. But when you are tempted, he will also provide a way out so that you can stand up under it.*
>
> 1 Corinthians 10:13

> *Consider it pure joy, my brothers, whenever you face trials of many kinds, because you know that the testing of your faith develops perseverance. Perseverance must finish its work so that you may be mature and complete, not lacking anything.*
>
> James 1:2-4

Note

1. David Seamands, *Healing for Damaged Emotions* (Wheaton, Ill.: Victor Books, 1981), page 30.

The NavPress Booklet Series includes:

A Woman of Excellence
by Cynthia Heald

Avoiding Common Financial Mistakes
by Ron Blue

Building Your Child's Self-Esteem
by Gary Smalley & John Trent

Dealing with Desires You Can't Control
by Mark R. McMinn

God Cares About Your Work
by Doug Sherman & William Hendricks

Hope for the Hurting
by Doug Sparks

How to Deal with Anger
by Dr. Larry Crabb

How to Handle Stress
by Don Warrick

How to Have a Quiet Time
by Warren & Ruth Myers

**How to Keep Your Head Up
When Your Job's Got You Down**
by Doug Sherman

How to Know God's Will
by Charles Stanley

How to Make Friends
by Jerry & Mary White

How to Overcome Loneliness
by Elisabeth Elliot

Prayer: Beholding God's Glory

When You Disagree: Resolving Marital Conflicts
by Jack & Carole Mayhall

You Can Trust God
by Jerry Bridges

Your Words Can Make a Difference
by Carole Mayhall